HOLY SPIRIT

In Transit

L. Charles Richerson

HOLY SPIRIT

In Transit

L. Charles Richerson

Holy Spirit in Transit
by L. Charles Richerson

Printed in the United States of America

Library of Congress Control Number: 2002111277
ISBN 1-591602-11-4

Richerson Enterprises
P.O. Box 51
Mukilteo, Washington 98275

Printed by Richerson Enterprises
First Printing 2002

Xulon Press
11350 Random Hills Road
Suite 800
Fairfax, VA 22030
(703) 279-6511
XulonPress.com

To order additional copies,
call 1-866-909-BOOK (2665).

ACKNOWLEDGEMENT

First, I thank Almighty God who created all things and without Him we would not have a reason to live.

Second, I thank His Son, Jesus Christ, who was sent to earth to be the salvation of all mankind of the world.

Third, I give thanks to the Holy Spirit for leading me into all truth and into His strength.

Fourth, I want to thank God for my darling wife, Edie, who encouraged me to write and helped me put together this book.

Lastly, I thank God for Julia whose growth in

Jesus Christ inspired me to share these stories with the world.

CONTENTS

PREFACE

During the past 30 years, I have driven a transit coach in several different cities in the United States. I am a Black man by birth, but a Bible-believing, Holy Spirit filled, and child of God with no skin color as far as God is concerned. (I Samuel 16:7) Some say I have the gift of faith and that is evidenced by my belief of the Bible. Sometimes I have been criticized by other Christians because I believe what is in the Bible. If God said it, then I believe it. I have been described as an exhorter and evangelist who can encourage people to do what they think they cannot do. I am a people person and love people. I like to see people succeed in life. I have always liked to read books. My favorite books are on wisdom and how to live a good life. But the interesting part is to read about all kinds of people who have overcome many types of situations in their lives by applying God's Word. However the Holy Bible is the best book that I have ever read on the subject of life and how to live it properly.

During my years of being a Christian and having learned to live by the Holy Spirit's moving in my life, my greatest joy is to tell people about what God has done for me and how He has a plan for each individual's life. (Jeremiah 29:10-13) Each day I ask God to send me someone to minister to and help to know God. For those who don't know who the Holy Spirit is, you will come to know without a doubt who He is.

Who is this Holy Spirit you might ask? He comes from the Almighty Living God, who, by the way, created you and gives you the very air that you breathe so you can live. The Holy Spirit lives in the heart of everyone who believes that Jesus Christ is the Son of the one true God and has trusted Him as their only Savior. If any of you dare to want to know about the Holy Spirit and His power, get the Holy Bible and read about him in the New Testament.

The next step is to repent, be sorry and turn away from your sin, and allow the Lord Jesus

Christ to be the Lord and Savoir of your life. Then the Holy Spirit will come to live in your life and guide you into God's truth. (John 16:13) Before one can work with the Holy Spirit, there is a condition that needs to be met. It is that one must be filled with the Holy Spirit and allow Him to rule your life. "What for," you may ask? Well the stories that will follow will explain exactly what I'm talking about.

I can tell you what Jesus, through the Holy Spirit can do for you. He can set you free from the curse of the law which is poverty, sickness, and premature death. (Deuteronomy 28:15-67 and Galatians 3:13) He can break every kind of bondage that you are in. He will remove a demon from a person who is willing to have the demon cast out. He may tell you to cast out a demon with just a word from Him and our obedience. Jesus said that to cast out some other evil spirits, you have to pray and fast. (Matthew 17:21) This takes time and preparation. God wants to use you, through the leading of the Holy Spirit, to be a blessing to the person that He brings to you. In the process you will receive a blessing as will the person you are praying for and helping.

Since you know by now, all of these stories involve my career as a bus driver, try to get a picture of the many people I came across while driving. There were all kinds of people from all kinds of races. For me it was a real education about people. There are a lot of sad and hurting people that you may not think were hurting until you got to know them better. I tried to be friendly with everyone. As a result, I learned that after people knew you really cared about them, they would open up and tell you about things they would not tell anyone else. This worked very well with me, because I could talk about Jesus, what He could do for them and how He could help them change their life for the better.

When I checked my bus out of the yard each day, I would pray the blood of Jesus over the bus, over each seat on the bus and over each individual that would board the bus. I would invite the Holy Spirit to be present on the bus and pray that each of the passengers would feel the Holy Spirit's presence on the bus. I would place my Bible on the dash board by the steering wheel to use when I needed it.

I'm writing this book because I know it will help someone out there who is hurting. Someone who is reading this may have lost a love one or is having trouble with their family. Others may be addicted to drugs or alcohol or have those who you love dearly addicted and they seem to have no hope of stopping. Maybe someone you know is sexually active and destroying their life, having no respect for themselves or anyone else. I've got good news for you. Help is not on its way, but HELP IS ALREADY HERE.

In this book, you will see how God prepares you for each new task that He has for you to perform. He, through the Holy Spirit, will educate and train you in preparation for the new task. What you will see also, is that He does not always use the same means to reach people. He, through the Holy Spirit, will prompt you in different ways to minister to the people He leads to you. One time He will prompt you to minister to a person in one way, the next time, he will give you a different way to minister to a different person. Sometimes we are moved by the Holy Spirit to plant a seed of salvation in a person, never seeing them make the actual decision to trust in God. Other times we are asked to lead the person to God after others have planted the seed of salvation in them. Still other times we only are prompted to encourage the person in the ways of God. No matter what way He chooses to use us, we must be sensitive to the leadings and promptings of the Holy Spirit to witness successfully to people. He will give you the words to say and prepare you for each encounter. (Mark 13:11)

I take no credit for any healing or miracles or life changes performed in these stories. God does the work and I have the faith and obedience.

So I say to you who are reading this book, *take note*. These stories are all true and are about the power of the Holy Spirit. They prove without a doubt that anyone can change their life, if they want to no matter what their age.

SEVEN YEARS OLD

Today was a beautiful day in the month of May. I was driving along a road in the outskirts of town. The weather was about 58 degrees with a light breeze. On this particular bus route there were not many passengers, so I could talk to a passenger for quite a while before I made a stop for anyone else to board or deboard. A middle aged lady, about thirty years old, asked me if I was a Christian. I said that I was and this question opened up a conversation between us that others could hear.

A young boy, seven years of age, rode my bus everyday going home from school. Each day when the little boy would board my bus I would say, "Hi." He would say, "Hi." right back.

The boy would sit in the front seat, looking straight at me as I was talking. The same people rode the bus at the same time everyday on this particular route. Day after day this same lady asked me to explain some things about Jesus Christ. I was more than willing to share. What I didn't realize was the little boy sitting across from me in the front seat was hearing every word that was spoken.

Now get ready for this move of the Holy Spirit on this young boy's life. On this particular day, in my spirit a voice said, "Lead this boy to salvation. Lead him to Jesus now."

When I felt this in my spirit I didn't want to do it. Why not? I'm a born again Christian. At this time in my life, I thought I would have to get this young boy to church for the pastor or somebody in the church to lead him to be saved, but not me! Please don't think this is weird. I believe that all people have these same conflicting feelings inside of themselves at one time or another, telling you to do or not to do something. How we respond is our choice.

But let's get back to our story. All this happened in a flash inside me. At this same time, the young boy got up out of the seat. I was relieved thinking I was going to get out of this; but, to my shock, the little boy said, "I have been listening to you talk about this Jesus and I want to know about Him."

Guess what? As we were talking, the little boy forgot to ring the bell to get off at his stop. Now there is no way out of this for me. I was nervous to say the least and I still had about five passengers on the bus. A couple of them would ride to the end of the line and come back with me to get off on the other side of the street because of traffic. So what was I to do?

At the end of the line I got up out of my seat and politely asked the passengers to stand out side the bus for a moment. I told them I need to talk to this boy in private. They agreed and left.

I began explaining to the young boy about who Jesus is and how He died for the whole world. I searched through my Bible and found a pamphlet I had been reading. Written on the back of the pamphlet was the Sinner's Prayer. In the next few minutes I led him in the Sinner's Prayer and he received Jesus as his Lord and Savoir. He looked so very happy. I felt his joy and was pleased with myself because I was obedient to do what the Holy Spirit had asked me to do. He even provided the Sinner's Prayer for me to use.

After we finished, I called back the people who stepped outside of the bus and we went on our way. As I was driving along, in my mind I keep thinking "God you are a miracle worker."

A few days passed and I didn't see the young boy anymore. I began to fear that maybe he told his parents and they were angry with me. Maybe they would complain about me to my company and my job would be in jeopardy. But I have come to find out when the Holy Spirit asks you to do something you don't you worry about the outcome. God will take care of you if you are obedient to His calling. So let's get back to the story.

A few days later, the young boy was at the bus stop where I normally picked him up. He seemed so happy and excited to see me as he came running to the door of the bus. When I realized that he was alright, I felt really good. But I had a great surprise coming.

As the little fellow stood in the doorway, he asked me to come see his mother because she wanted to talk to me. I looked outside the bus to see if I could see his mother and there, parked in a car next to the bus, was a lady that was waving at me. Getting up from my seat, I went outside to see this lady. She introduced herself as the little boy's mother and began speaking to me. I must admit to you her words were like music to my ears. She said to me in a most gracious tone of voice almost crying, "What did you tell my son? He has changed over night. He behaves better, his teachers at school say he has changed. I want to thank you. My husband and I can't believe how he has changed so quickly."

In my humble way I explained that he heard me talking about Jesus on the bus and wanted to know this Jesus. Explaining further how I had told him about Jesus, I recited how the Holy Spirit told me to lead her son to salvation in Jesus Christ. Afterward he had prayed and accepted Jesus into his heart.

She was very appreciative and continued to thank me. I explained that it was God that had made the change in her son. I had just told him about God.

In the Bible, Jesus himself says "...for with God all things are possible." (Mark 10:27) Think about this statement for a moment. Look at your life right now. Do you want to change yourself or change the way things are in your life? Well I've got good news for you. JESUS IS THE WAY. Whatever it was that caused the little boy to act the way he did before he knew Jesus, he has been set FREE. And you too can be set free, whoever you are.

PREJUDICE REMOVED

This next story will show the reader the softening power the Holy Spirit of God. I parked my bus at one of the malls in the city. As people began to board my bus, a young man about the age of eighteen or nineteen years old walked through the door and put his fare in the fare box. He was white male about five feet nine inches tall with dark hair, dressed in an army-type camouflage shirt and pants and wore black high-top laced boots. He carried some carpenter tools that caused me to believe he had a job somewhere. What made him different from most of my passengers was that he never spoke to anyone on the bus. He never spoke to me as he boarded the bus. I said, "Good afternoon." to him many times, but he never said a word to me. The expression on his face was one of deep anger. From my past observations and by his behavior and dress, I thought that he may be a white supremacist activist. Let's call him Tom, which is not his real name, but changed for his protection, which you will understand later on in the story.

I continued to be friendly to all my passengers because I was taught if you want friends, you have to be friendly.

After almost two weeks of Tom riding my bus without ever saying a word, I felt bold enough to reach out to him. As he was getting up out of his seat to leave the bus, I said to him, "I would like to shake your hand, because I have been watching you for over a week and you appear to be going to work. Every day, you are always on time and I respect that, especially in a teenager." I looked at him straight in the eye and continued, "There are so many teenagers wasting their life away just hanging around, but not you." I finished by telling him my name.

All the time I was saying this to him my hand was extended to him, but he was hesitant to touch my hand. As he listened to me, a strange thing began to take place in him. He reached for my hand as if he couldn't help himself and shook it, although he really didn't want to shake it. He did not respond to my statement but got off the bus.

As I drove on, I thought about him and what was probably going on in his mind. What he had done by shaking my hand seemed to be something new for him. I was right, because the next day, an unusual thing happened. When I parked at the bus stop at the mall, which I did five days a week, nobody was there. All of a sudden there came Tom. No one else was around but him. He got on the bus and this time he said, "Hello." and sat down on the front seat, something he had never done before. He always sat in the back of the bus.

"Hello." I responded. Today there was something different about him. I was eager to hear about it. No other passenger came near the bus for about seven minutes.

He told me his name and continued by saying, "I come from a family who has white supremacist views. My whole family is full of hate. I was taught to hate Blacks, Jews, and all minorities. You are the first Black man I have ever shaken hands with." He went on explaining how he felt and I listened intently as he spoke from his heart. "I watched you everyday as you talked to people. You are friendly with all races, no matter what they look like, or what race they are. It doesn't seem to matter to you how they are dressed. How did you get that way?" Then he continued in a most truthful sounding voice, "I'm tired of hating."

Now stop for a moment and pause. Let what he said sink into your mind. What was causing him to change? He had seen love and joy demonstrated between people of all races and he wanted to experience that same love and joy.

"I got this way by believing in Jesus Christ as my Lord and Savior. Jesus is in the business of saving and changing lives." I replied boldly.

Explaining to him that he needed to give his life to Jesus, I told him to then find a good Bible-believing church that believes that Jesus is the Son of God, and practices all the fruits of the Holy Spirit found in Galatians 5:22. I described how he would learn about Jesus that He died for all mankind to set them free from all kinds of bondage, including prejudice. I told him he would have support from people in the church, and would learn how to walk in righteousness.

Later Tom told me he had found a church and made Jesus his Lord and Savior. His life and activities changed.

This may sound like a great end to this story, but not just yet. A few weeks later, as I pulled my bus up to the bus stop, there were about seven teenagers that had surrounded Tom ready to attack him. I couldn't understand what I was seeing. These teenagers were multiracial; Blacks, Whites, and Mexicans together, all with shaved heads and out to get Tom. This was very confusing to me. I had to act quickly or maybe they would beat Tom up, maybe even kill him. A white male friend of mine and I jumped out of the bus and ran between the teenagers and Tom.

"Stop this." I told them. "What are you guys doing?"

One of the teenagers said, "Tom is a racist. He and his family hate Jews, Blacks, and all minorities." The teenagers went on to tell about the fights Tom had at school. One time he beat up a Black girl, and now they were here to teach him a lesson.

I spoke up quickly and said, "No you are not." I told my friend to go call the police quick.

One of the teenagers asked me, "Why are you taking up for this racist? You're Black."

"Tom has changed." I said. "He doesn't believe that way anymore."

They didn't look convinced, but stopped advancing toward Tom. I stayed between them and Tom and continued to talk. They weren't convinced but left before the police arrived. I filled out a police report and was asked to go the police station to talk to a certain officer.

The next day at the police station, I asked the officer if there was a multiracial teenage gang operating in this area. To my surprise he said there was and the police had been following their activities for some time. I shook my head in disbelief. He explained that they had been active in this city and in another to the north. He was glad for my intervention in the situation.

Several days later, Tom told me that he had to find another place to live because his parents told him to get out of their house. They didn't want to hear all of his Christian talk and didn't like the change they had seen in his attitude. He explained there were a lot of people in this town who didn't know that he was a Christian now and there was too much trouble for him here. He had to find another city to start over again. I gave him my blessing and told him God would take care of him. He shook my hand and said, "Thanks for everything."

I replied, "You are more than welcome."

It was sad to see him leave that way. I knew him only a very short time, but I considered him a friend.

No matter what we do in life, we all reap

what we sow. (Galatians 6:7) There are consequences for the choices we make. But Tom was fortunate to want to change. He now has a new beginning, a new birth in Jesus Christ. His past sins are forgiven and Tom has a great new future ahead and we wish him well.

SATAN UNMASKED

This day on the road as I traveled along, the weather was warm and there was a little breeze. I even opened the side window of the bus to feel the air. On this trip I didn't pick up many passengers. To tell the truth I was enjoying being alone at this particular time because time alone on the bus was time spent talking to God and being led by the Holy Spirit.

Soon up the road I could see two passengers waiting to board the bus, a male and female. They looked to be about the age twenty or twenty years old. I found out later they were both only eighteen years old. Now let's begin their story.

The young lady was dressed in a short mini

skirt, tight sweater, thick-soled black boots, and earrings in her ears, about six or eight of them. Her hair was black and spiked. (For those who don't know what spiked hair looks like, when you look at the person's head, it looks as if the person has been shocked with electricity.) Every one of her fingers had a ring on it, and her fingernails were painted black. She wore black lipstick, and black eye shadow. The young man with her was medium build, about five feet eleven inches tall; a little taller than his girlfriend. He had black hair, wore black pants, black shirt, black leather overcoat, and black shoes.

In my mind I thought, "These people must have heard the statement that Black people say, "Black is beautiful." In this case, they went all out! But I was wrong. They had another reason to dress this way. What was it?

I was to find out the reason was rebellion, hurt, disappointment, and lots of anger. I noticed right away that the young man was carrying a book with him. He held the book in a way that he purposely wanted me to see it. I surely did see it because it was Satan's bible.

You see, I carry my Bible on the bus with me, because I'm not ashamed to be a Christian anywhere that I may be. Plus I might have to answer questions someone may have about my belief. Having the Bible right there with me, they wouldn't have to take my word for it. I could show them on the spot what God says in His Word. And, oh boy. I didn't know that the opportunity would come so soon.

The couple went to the back of the bus and took their seats. In about two minutes the Holy Spirit very quietly told me to call the young man back up to the front and minister to him. When the Holy Spirit wants you to do something don't ever worry about doing it. He will give you the words and lead you.

Calling the young man up to the front of the bus, I introduced myself and asked him his name. He told his name was Robert. His girlfriend followed him up to the front also. She said her name was Kate.

After the introductions, I boldly asked him about his book. He said with real conviction and eyeing my Bible, "This is the satanic bible, and I believe in it. I don't believe in God."

The Holy Spirit can do a mighty work on a mind that is living in darkness. Because it is the truth that will set you free. Lies of the devil will keep you in bondage. Now you, who are reading this, pay close attention.

I said to Robert, "You really don't believe in

God?"

He said, "No. I believe in the devil and there is no God."

"Who told you that?" I asked.

He said, "Satan says it."

Looking him in the eye I said, "Satan has deceived you because he believes and knows that there is a God. He even talked to God's son, Jesus Christ, in the New Testament of the Bible. Isn't it strange that the devil tells you not to believe in God but in reality he himself believes in God? Why would he do that?" They both looked shocked and bewildered.

I pulled the bus over at the next stop. "Look here in my Bible," I continued. "I will show you so you can see for yourself." I opened the Bible to James 2:19 and Matthew 4:1-11. They both read the verses. Watching them was like seeing air coming out of a balloon. They didn't want to believe what they were reading. They didn't say a word but went back to their seats with a puzzled look on their faces. In the mirror above I could see them talking together in the back of the bus. I knew that their belief system was shattered to pieces.

The truth of God has a way of doing that to you when you hear and receive it, even though you don't want to believe it. It will haunt you. It will prove to you that whatever you build in life, won't last if you don't build it with God.

As the week went on, Robert and Kate continued to ride my bus everyday. We talked about the Bible and Jesus. Robert and Kate were not "street" people. They were from broken families, but had someone who loved them and provided for them. At the time, Robert was living with Kate and her mother. After a while I invited them to my church.

After telling my wife about them, we set a date to pick them up. When my wife saw them for the first time, she was a little intimidated. I couldn't blame her, because their dress resembled Halloween costumes. I don't say that to condemn them, but their dress code would be considered extreme.

As a Christian who follows Jesus, we don't look at the outside or the clothing of a person. Since we have the mind of Christ, He wants us to see the person as a soul that God loves. (I Samuel 16:7) It is their soul that God wants to save and give them a new birth. I have seen many people who have made a mistake and would like to start over but they feel so much guilt. They don't believe God or people will forgive them, so they just go on living the low life. If there are any of you who are reading these true stories right now who feel this way, give your life to Jesus right now. He will forgive you if you ask Him. Turn away from your life style that can only destroy you.

Continuing with the story, my wife and I picked up Robert and Kate Sunday morning and arrived at church about 9:45 am. We took them to our Sunday School Class after the regular service. Sorry to say our church was not very friendly toward them. The church folk were overly polite to them in a phony way. I'm sure Robert and Kate knew it to.

After the service, we took Robert and Kate to our house for a good meal continued talking to them. We had three teenagers at the time that joined in our discussions. After a time of visiting, we took them back home.

We never invited them back to the church and they didn't ask to come back. (A short time later, we started attending a different church, one that reflects our acceptance of people as they are. It is a church that is very friendly to new people and is very interested in helping people to be saved.)

In the days that followed, I would see Robert and Kate on the bus and continued to show them love and respect. Robert told me that he and his father had not talked to each for eight years.

After hearing the word of God as I revealed it to him, he wanted to change. In the days that followed, he cut his hair, changed his style of clothing and got a good job.

Kate was still very angry inside. She hated her mother and she did not like the way that Robert had changed. She tried hard to keep him as he had been. She wanted to control him. You must understand Kate was unhappy and wanted Robert to stay unhappy with her.

But thank God, Robert was strong enough to know that the life style he had led was no good. He wanted no part of it anymore. Robert finally saved enough money to go back to California to visit his father and to make amends.

As for Kate, the last I saw her she still seemed to be searching for that real peace that you won't find in the world. That peace is only found in God, through Jesus Christ. Kate will turn to Jesus one day when she gets tired and fed up with Satan and his lies.

A QUICK ENCOUNTER

This next story is a story of two brothers that I met on my bus route. It will reveal how the Holy Spirit works in relation to time. Sometimes when the Holy Spirit works, the results are instant, but at other times there is a period of waiting before you may see any results.

This day was going along fine. There was nothing special out of the ordinary until I saw two young men standing at the next bus stop. As I got closer I could see that they were high on drugs or intoxicated with alcohol. These young men were about seventeen or eighteen years old. They were nice looking and I thought what a waste to be destroyed so by drugs.

In the years of my life, I have seen many young lives lost to drugs. I hate drugs because I have seen what can happen when you mess with it. A cousin of mine was turned on to drugs and overdosed at thirteen years of age. When I was young I went to parties where almost everyone there was taking drugs. One girl I knew tried to get me to take some by kissing me, hoping to put some in my mouth, but it didn't work. I am the kind of guy that doesn't have to try everything to know if it is good or not. Being able to learn very easily by watching other people's mistakes, I never did take any drugs. When I see other people dieing from taking drugs and, if I value my life, I would consider myself a fool to take the risk. You should understand by now how I feel about drugs. It hurts when I see young people ruining their lives on drugs.

Let's get on with the story. As I stopped the bus and looked at these two young men staggering in onto the bus, I was angry. They could hardly stand and were fumbling in their pockets to get money to pay their fare. I told them in a loud voice to sit down over in the front seat. They managed to sit down. The people on the bus were surprised to hear me speak loudly. Everything was quiet for a brief moment. I began to drive on to the mall.

You must understand I wasn't angry at them but angry at the devil. He is the enemy that deceives the world. The Bible says that he (the thief) is the one that comes to kill, steal, and destroy. Jesus came to give us life and to give it more abundantly. (John 10:10) The Bible says we Christians can be angry but do not sin. (Ephesians 4:26) I began to drive on down the road, but I could not keep quiet.

I asked the two young men, "Why do you want to destroy your lives? You've got so much life ahead ofyou. You both are strong young men with the whole world out there waiting for you. Why are you messing with drugs? Jesus died on the cross for you. He loves and wants the best for you. Don't throw your life away like this. Get yourselves together. Straighten your life up and do something positive. If you keep going like this, you will die early, or end up in some prison."

They just looked at me with a dazed look. I explained to them,

"I'm talking to you both this way because I love you, and don't want to see your life to go down the drain because of drugs. Wake up and get in the business of living."

I said all this in about five minutes but didn't see any response on their faces. It was like my words hit a stone wall. They were so stoned I don't see how they made it to the bus stop. But they could see well enough to ring the bell to get off at the next stop. They both staggered to get up and left. I felt compassion for them because my wife and I had teenagers and we knew how a parent would feel with wayward children.

For the rest of the day as I drove, I kept thinking about those two young men. I prayed that God would somehow touch them. The great lesson I learned that day was that when we reach out to someone to help them and don't see any response right away, don't think that the seed you have planted hasn't taken root. Let me demonstrate.

About two or three years later, my wife and I were walking in a mall near our home. We were looking at all the nice things and taking our time. It was a beautiful day with a lot of people out shopping. As we continued to walk slowly along, just a few feet ahead of us was a young man and a young lady pushing a little baby in a stroller.

When we had just about passed each other, the young man said as he was turning in our direction, "Hey. Don't you remember me?"

I turned and looked at him but couldn't place him. He started telling us that he and his brother got on my bus one day. He remembered that I was preaching to them about drugs and I had told them to get their life together. I looked at him again and this time I recognized him. Wow! He was sober, but what he said next was the icing on the cake. He explained that he taken my advice, gone to church and given his life to Jesus. Since then, he had met this fine Christian lady and had been married and this was their baby. He went on to say that his brother had given his life to Jesus, too.

My heart was just bubbling with joy inside. As I said earlier, I didn't think they heard a word I said, but somehow the Holy Spirit's power got through to them. Praise the Lord! That's not all, there is more.

The church that my wife and I attend to has two services on Sunday morning. So guess what? After asking the young man and his wife what church they attend, come to find out they go to our church, only at a different time. He even sang in a youth music group there. Can you believe that? We never saw each other. What an amazing discovery.

It proves that when we are talking to someone, we may not see any reaction to our words from the outer appearance, but the Holy Spirit is working on the inside. The Apostle Paul said that some may plant the seed, some may water, and some may see the increase. (I Corinthians 3:6 & 7) This story is a good example of this verse.

FROM DARKNESS TO LIGHT

This story shows how God, through the Holy Spirit, can change a life over a period of time. It begins with a young female teenager. She rode my bus every week to school. A good looking young lady with black hair and dark eyes, her clothes were quite bold and somewhat revealing and along with black lipstick and fingernail polish, she displayed what you might call the "punk rock" look. I could sense that behind all this, there was a hurting young lady that was looking for something that she needed, but did not know what it was. She was seeking love and peace, but in all the wrong places. Don't put the book down yet! Read on and find out where this young lady found love and peace.

When she got off the bus, her friends, dressed similarly, were waiting for her. They all *seemed* happy but it wasn't a real happiness. They all seemed to be hiding something underneath. It was pain, hurt and disappointment of some type, I learned later. The truth of the matter was they were not really as happy as they appeared. The question is: What can be done about it? I have seen miracles performed in people's lives, even in my family's lives; so I am confident God can help these teens too.

After awhile, this young lady and I began to talk about all kinds of things, including her hopes and goals. As I continued to pick her up on the bus, she developed a kind of respect for me in a shameful way. Later she told me that she would not get "high" on marijuana if she knew she would be riding the bus with me because she did not want me to see her in her "high" state. I knew that she had been "high" on something when I first met her. But let me remind you, I never said anything about the way she dressed or condemned her in any way. What I did was to show her that she was special in God's eyes. That He loved her so much that He sent His Son, Jesus Christ, to die for her and the whole world to set us FREE! Free from the lies the devil, our fleshly desires, and all the things the world's ways would try to draw us into. What happened next only the Holy Spirit could do.

This particular morning, when the young lady boarded my bus, we exchanged the usual the greetings of, "Good morning." "How are you today?" In my heart the Holy Spirit said to me, "Tell her this. "You don't have to live this way, you are better than this.""

So, in obedience, I told her this and immediately her expression changed. She looked confused but still interested in my comment. The seed of rebirth was planted. What do I mean by that statement? Read on and see.

I continued talking to her about how God loved her and had a plan for her life. She listened as I explained how she could ask Jesus into her heart and have her whole life change for the better. She confided in me that she felt she needed a change in her life.

Later on, my wife and I invited her and her boyfriend to our church. I didn't know her boyfriend, but he dressed "punk" like her. When a person thinks they have found something really good, they want their friends or love ones to share in it. She wanted him to share her longing for something different.

At the end of the service, while the invitation to be saved was being given, the young lady tried to get her boyfriend to go down the aisle with her, but he would not. She went down to the alter and gave her life to the Lord Jesus Christ. We church folks call this being "born again" as Jesus did in John 3:3.

She immediately felt a great burden lifted from her shoulders and the peace she was longing for had flooded her spirit. She now had eternal life, and this world with the lies and destruction have no claim on her life anymore. You would have to have seen her before she was saved to know the miraculous work that the Holy Spirit did and is still doing for her. She is living her life for God now and readily testifies to the changes God has performed in her life. She is studying toward a life in some area of ministry.

What happened to her boyfriend? The last thing she told me about him was that he wanted to live his life his way. They have since broken up and gone their own ways.

When we are going through a life with many struggles, and we are not fulfilled; when there is still emptiness after all the offering of parties and fleshly desires; when we struggle over and over again, we are being taught that what we are doing doesn't work. We need to change directions. The Holy Spirit is waiting for YOU! Jesus Christ is the door. He himself said, "Come unto me, all you who are heavy laden, and I will give you rest." (Matthew 11:28) "I have come that they may have life and that they may have it more abundantly." (John 10:10)

The young lady in the story you have just read is enjoying this life with Jesus now. SO CAN YOU!

ALMOST

This story is not easy for me to tell because the person was on the right track to being changed for the better, but because of the past mistakes that both he and his wife had made, faith could not work. You who are reading these stories must understand this. Faith will not work if you are full of fear. Whatever you give your attention to, will be your life experience. Jesus said Matthew 12:37, "By your words you will be justified and by your words you will be condemned." This story will prove to you how true this is.

This story starts out at night about 8:30 pm. I was driving along my route with three passengers on the bus. They were going home after working late on their jobs. Some were even taking a short nap. If they fell into a deep sleep I would wake them since I knew which bus stop was theirs. Traffic on the street was light. Just up ahead at the next bus stop I could see a passenger standing alone. When I pulled up and stopped, there stood a shaggy looking man wearing a long overcoat and gloves with holes in them. He stood about 5 feet 8 inches and maybe about 160 lbs. in weight. He was out-right dirty.

As he stood outside the open door of the bus and asked if I was going to 76th Street, the smell of alcohol drifted into the bus. As I said that I was going there he boarded the bus. He explained that he didn't have any money to pay and I told him that was alright. He thanked me for the free ride.

I started a conversation with him and asked him why he was living like this. He said that he was an alcoholic and was going to a meeting where others like him were trying to get help to stop drinking. As he talked on about his condition, I felt compassion for him. He really didn't like the way he was, but alcohol had him in bondage.

I don't claim to be an expert on human behavior or a psychologist, but when you see people deep in drugs or drinking there is some cause that is even deeper. As we were nearing his stop, I asked him if he was going to ride my bus again. I wanted to see him again so I could talk to him about Jesus. He said that he could be back tomorrow night. I asked him what his name was. As he told me I shook his hand and he disappeared into the night. I wondered if I would really see him again. The rest of the night I keep thinking about the man with the drinking problem. I asked God to give me wisdom to help him if I saw him again.

Behold the next night there he was. He seemed glad to see me again. I always greet and respect every passenger that enters my bus and it was no different with him. He even told me that I was different from other bus drivers because I treated him kindly. What he didn't know was it wasn't me; it was the Spirit of Jesus that he saw in me.

After a couple of meetings on the bus I asked him to come to church with my wife and me. He said that he would. I asked for his address and told him what time we would pick him up on Sunday.

I told my wife about him and Sunday morning we went to the address he had given me. It was in a neighborhood known for drug dealing. I went up the steps and knocked on the door. The young man came to the door looking cleaned up and better dressed. He lived in a small apartment with his wife and little girl. He introduced me to them and we left.

As we walked down the steps, he told me he had been living on the street. He had told his wife that he wanted to change and make their marriage work. So she had let him come back into their home. I told him we had room in the car if his wife and daughter wanted to come to church, too. He said she didn't want to go because she wasn't dressed right.

At the church many people greeted him as we went in. Our new church is known for its friendliness and warm welcome to anyone who comes. He listened intently during the service. As we left the church, the young man made the statement that he really liked our church. He went on to say that he had been in other churches and the folks acted like they didn't really want him there. He said after attending other churches he felt worse when he came out than he had felt when he went in. But our church was different. He felt uplifted and happy when he came out of our church.I understood what he meant. Some church folks want you to look like them and dress like them, otherwise you don't fit in. I thank God that Jesus is not like that. Jesus receives you just as you are. He came to earth and died for all of us, no matter what we look like or dress like. After we dropped the young man off at his apartment, my wife and I talked about the young man on the way home. We could see that he enjoyed our church and were sure he would return.

The next Sunday, as we picked him up again, we reminded him that his wife and little daughter were welcome to come along with him. We explained that our church had a very good Sunday school class for his daughter.

A few weeks later, after some persuasion, his wife decided to come with us to church. The young man was excited for his family to be with him and I could see that he was really trying to turn his life around. On the other hand, his wife didn't seem to want to try to make things better. She and the little daughter came with him for several Sundays but, in the car, she would continually remind her husband of the things he had done in the past week that had not pleased her. To gain sympathy for herself, it seemed like she wanted us to know the wrong things he had been doing.

One Sunday when I went to pick them up to go to church, I heard them shouting and quarreling with one another. This time he came to church without his wife. My wife and I learned later she didn't trust him anymore. She had told him that he had disappointed her in the past with his drinking and drugs. She just kept talking about all the bad things he had done.

In a meeting with her later, my wife and I told her she had to forgive him. God would help her if she was willing. She said that she couldn't forgive him or forget what he had done. She continued to tell us of the hurtful things he had done in the past. She never had anything good to say about him or even commend him for trying to make their marriage work.

I could see the young man was trying, but in a short time he moved back out onto the streets and went back to drinking heavily. His wife and daughter continued to come to church for a short time because the daughter really liked the Sunday school class. Finally she called to tell us that she was that she was going to move back to some other state to live. We never saw them again.

The opportunity for a new life was before them to receive, but past hurts prevented them from the life Jesus came to give them. The words that come out of our mouths are seeds that will produce our futures. We can prove it to ourselves. Listen to people who complain all the time about their life and want to blame everybody for their condition. Check it out. Then listen to the people who have peace and prosperity. They talk different. One group talks about what they CAN'T DO! The other one group says "HOW CAN WE DO THIS!" Jesus was correct when He said we can have whatever we say. But we must forgive our brothers or sisters of their sins so God can forgive us our sins. (Mark 11:24 & 25)

Come to God and He will help you in all things. There is nothing impossible WITH GOD! (Matthew 19:26) The couple in this story ALMOST got it. But we all know that ALMOST DOESN'T COUNT.

ENERGY REDIRECTED

These next stories show how all of life is energy, and the way we direct it, can be good or evil. In this segment I will be telling two stories.

About twice a year our bus company allows the drivers to pick different routes. This is called a "shakeup" and gives the driver a chance to pick another route for different scenery, or to see different people, or just because their tired of the same old route. It's a good thing for some drivers. The drivers pick runs by seniority. So, because you are down the line in seniority, you may get a route that no one wants or a route that the driver before you had a bad experience with the passengers. This happens from time to time. I'm ok with any route because I have the Holy Spirit with me. You readers know by now that when He rides with me, it won't matter what route I have.

Well guess what? I got one of those routes. I picked up young teenagers that attend an alternate school because they are incompatible with and don't behave in the regular schools. These teenagers are known to be disruptive and hard to handle. For some of them, this is their last hope to try to get a decent education before they go out into the real world. Let me tell you, if you don't have some kind of education about the world and its ways, experiences will teach you the hard way. But you learn one way or another.

The first story is one about a young teenager, let's call him Tom. Tom was about 17 years old, medium build, 5ft 7 tall, dark hair. He was a nice looking young man and had a lot of energy, but he used it in the wrong way and got into a lot of trouble at this school. They expelled him out of the regular school and sent him to this alternate school to try to salvage him. To me he seemed like he just needed to direct his energy in the right place. I first saw him at the bus stop at an hour when he was supposed to be in school. When I picked him up, I asked him, "Is there school today?"

He replied, "I got kicked out of school today.

I'm suspended for three days."

"Suspended for what?" I asked. He explained that he liked to tear things up. There are fire extinguishers in the hall way at the school. He said he liked to pull them off the wall and spray them all over the place.

I looked at him and said, "Don't you know that type of behavior will get you in trouble with the school?"

Without any remorse he said, "Yeah."

I told him very sternly, "Don't you know that if you keep up this kind of behavior it will eventually lead to trouble or even get you put away in jail or prison?"

He looked puzzled. He paused for a moment and said to me in a very sincere voice, "I can't help it. I just like to destroy things."

Tom really meant what he was saying. I wanted to help him so badly, but I didn't know what to say to him. The Holy Spirit knew. He is in the business of helping people. I'm not telling you readers anything you don't know already, right? So the very next moment I told him, by the leading of the Holy Spirit, "Did you know that you can get paid good money for destroying things?"

He looked surprised, and said, "No I didn't."

I said, "They are called Demolitionists. They

are workers that destroy big buildings, bringing them down with dynamite, and big bulldozers. Tom, since you like to destroy things, you can do it legally and get paid for it."

Tom got real excited when I told him this. While I was driving the bus, I kept talking to him and encouraging him. He was supposed to get off, but I had his attention. The Holy Spirit speaking through me, was giving him the answer to his problem. I told him to go to the library and ask the clerk to help him find books about training to be worker who demolishes big buildings.

Tom looked at me with a big smile on his face and said, "I'm going to do it right now."

He soon got off the bus, thanked me and left. I felt really good that maybe I had helped one teenager to turn his life around. I was right because in a few days he got on the bus and said he was starting training to be, are you ready for this, a Demolitionist. He didn't waste any time. Remember he already had a lot of energy; he just needed to direct it in the right way. The Holy Spirit rides again!

The next story is similar to the last one. This young man was always skateboarding at the bus park and ride lot. I would see him every day doing the same thing. Now I don't believe there is anything wrong with skateboarding. But it was plain to see that the young man was not going to school because of the hours that I would see him. I'm big on learning and education. You need to know about life and how to live abundantly in this world. The Bible says to get wisdom, and in all to get understanding. (Proverbs 4:7) I'm not against having fun in life, but there is more to life than just having fun. We all have a purpose in life. Everyone has an assignment to help someone or to help some people. A dentist fixes teeth, a mechanic fix cars and so on.

I saw this young man day after day and I knew that there was something I could do to help him. He looked to be about only 16 years of age. Finally one day I drove my bus into the park and ride lot and, checking my watch, I found I had a little lay-over time. I got out of the bus and went over to the young man. He was just enjoying his skateboard. The truth of the matter was he wasn't supposed to skateboarding in the park and ride lot.

I have learned to respect all people, and treat them like I want to be treated. You can ask people to do almost anything if you ask them in the right way. It is the manor in which you ask them that produces the way they respond.

The first thing I said when I approached him

was, "Say. You are pretty good on that skateboard."

He looked at me with a big proud smile on his face and stopped skating. I asked him if I could talk to him for a minute. I politely told him to be careful on his skateboard because of the buses that come in this area. Continuing on I told him it was too bad there was not a place for the skateboarders to ride their skateboards so they wouldn't anger the general public. He agreed with me.

I asked him, "Why aren't you in school?"

He said without hesitation, "I don't like school."

"What don't you like about school?" I replied.

"I don't like the subjects they teach me." he explained.

I told him it would be a good idea for him to at least learn how to read and count money so no one could cheat him. That got a smile out of him.

Then I remembered there was a school that was located by our bus company that would take in teenagers and would give them a chance to learn a trade of their choice. What a great idea for this young teenager. In this school he would get to choose what he wanted to study.

In response to the Holy Spirit's leading, I told him about the school, wrote down the address for him and told him what bus to take to get there. I even gave him an all day bus pass, so he wouldn't need any money to get home. He took the pass and put it in his pocket. I wasn't too sure that he would take my advice. I left the park and ride lot praying that he would go, find something at this school that would get his attention, and pursue it.

It was my desire to see him again later, and to hear a good report from him. God did grant me that desire, for one day there he was standing at the park and ride lot. He had never ridden my bus before, so when he stepped up to enter the bus and saw me, he looked excited and I was surprised, too.

He said to me as he was putting his money in the fare box, "You don't remember me, do you?"

"Yes I do." I replied. "Go ahead and lay it on me." That's ghetto talk.

"I took your advice and went to that trade school you told me about." he said. As we drove away, he told me that he would soon be finished with the training to be a welder and the next week he had a job as an apprentice working as "on-the-job training" under another person. He couldn't believe that he would be making big money at this time in his young life.

"Well, congratulations. I'm very proud of

you." I encouraged. I continued to tell him that I knew he would make a good employee because he liked his new profession. When a person likes what they are doing, they make sure they get to work to do that work.

As he got off the bus he smiled and said, "Good by and thank you."

What a difference we can make in young person's life if we will just reach out to them and show them we care.

EIGHT YEARS OF PAIN

Here is a story that started in the university campus area. After driving many trips to the university campus you notice and meet all kinds of passengers. Then, in time, you may strike up a conversation with them. After awhile you get to know them and find out what their goal is in life. You learn a lot about people if you let them talk.

One day on the bus a lady about 40 years old, 5 feet 11 inches tall, medium build got on the bus with a cloth bag of books. These were not the kind of books that most of the college students carried. How do I know? When she went by me I looked into the bag and saw some of them. After a few trips on the bus I asked her where she got the books she carried. She told me that she worked at a book store. Well, that made sense.

Anyway we began to talk about a lot of things, and come to find out she was a born-again Christian. Great! She was married with a family and they all were doing well. Most people would say how nice. But what I didn't know was she had pain that would attack her body in the back of her neck almost every week. Here is the way I found it out.

One afternoon I picked her up at the bus stop, and when she stepped into the bus, I couldn't help but notice her skin color was a light shade of purple. She looked dizzy and sickly. I was really concerned for her. I motioned for her to sit down in the first seat where I could talk to her and said, "What is the matter? You don't look well. Can I call a Medic for you?"

She replied, "No". She went on to explain to me about this neck pain that kept coming back over and over again. She had endured it for the past eight years. She said that she took medication for it, but the pain still came back.

Guess what happened next? You are right. Again the Holy Spirit told me in His soft voice to ask her if she believed that Jesus could heal her neck. When I asked her that, she looked at me surprised that I would even ask that question knowing that she was a Christian. (Well, I know a few Christian people that don't believe that God still heals today, sorry to say.)

But she said, "Yes, I do believe God can heal me."

The Holy Spirit told me to tell her that tonight when she went to bed, to put her hand on the back of her neck where the pain is, and say these words, "Jesus I believe I'm healed." Explaining this to her, I also said that I would pray in agreement with her to cast out that pain. I reminded her that she must believe in faith that it would happen. She agreed and said she would do it.

After awhile her bus stop was just ahead. When she got up out of her seat, I shook her hand and told her not to worry. She looked very weak, but I knew God could heal her. I whispered a prayer for her as she left the bus and was relived when I looked out to see someone had come to pick her up at the bus stop.

I continued on my bus route until all my passengers were gone. I took this time to thank God for using me to help this lady. Since I was alone again, I could pray loudly thanking God for His awesome power of the Holy Spirit to heal. In my spirit I knew He could do it. My hope was that she would not let fear stop her from trusting in God.

When you read the Bible, you will find in many of the miracles that Jesus performed he said to the person, "Fear Not!" Jesus knows that fear is an enemy that can rob you of the blessings that God has already laid up for you!

After my shift was over, driving the bus back to the base, I was thinking how many people will live a life far below what God created them to live. It is God's will that we prosper and be in good health, as our soul prospers. (III John verse 2) It is not God's will for you to be sick or poor. Many things that we do ourselves or allow to happen to us can cause sickness or poverty to come upon us. In the year 2000 I almost died because of worry about my youngest son, but that's another story.

Let's get on with this one. The very next day on my trip coming out of the university campus, standing at the bus stop was the lady that I had prayed for the day before. She got on the bus smiled and this time she had to go to the back of the bus, because the front seats were full. Her skin was back to its normal color and she looked much better than the day before. After the ride on the freeway, I pulled into the park and ride lot. This was where she usually got off the bus, but she didn't get off this time.

At first I thought she may have forgotten. As I looked in my rear view mirror above me, it appeared like she knew where she was going. She had not forgotten her stop, so I continued on my route.

After arriving at my last stop which was another park and ride lot, all the people left except her. She asked me if she could ride the turn-around loop with me. She said that she wanted to tell me what happened to her last night. She seemed very excited to say the least! I was ready and expecting good news. And let me tell you I got it. Listen to this.

With just her and me on the bus, she sat down in the front seat. She began to explain that last night she did exactly as I told her to do; as the Holy Spirit had told me. She said, at 9:00 pm as she lay in bed she put her hand on the back of her neck and said the words I told her to say. When she touched her neck, a pain shot through her neck like nothing ever before. She could hardly stand it. But just a few seconds afterward it was completely gone. She began to cry tears of joy. She asked me what she could do for me to repay me. I told her that she could do nothing for me, but the reward that I got was to see God set people free. But she kept on trying to do something for me.

Finally she asked, "Would you and your wife come to our church for a Christmas dinner and program? I want you to meet my husband because I told him about you and he wants to thank you, too."

So I said I would talk to my wife and let her know tomorrow. Soon she got off the bus and was gone.

I was overjoyed by the way God healed her. One thing I found out about God, he doesn't heal the same way all the time. But one thing I can assure you, trust Him to do it. Have faith without doubt in your heart and Jesus said it will be done. Remember you must forgive any person about whom you have any anger or bad feelings. (Mark 11:23-26)

My wife and I went to the Christmas dinner and had a good time. Her husband was so appreciative of the things I had told his wife and to God for healing his wife. The lady continued to ride the bus and never again felt that pain that had her in bondage for eight years. Praise The Lord!

THE EPILEPTIC HEALED

It was a beautiful day in late September. The sun was shining bright as I was driving down the freeway going to town to take most of my passengers to the university. My bus was nearly full, and my passengers seemed to be in a happy mood. There is something to say about sunshine. It seems to bring out the best in people. After driving 30 years, carrying the public from place to place, I can truly say that the weather does have an affect on people's behavior. When it is cloudy weather, the people are more depressed and withdrawn, but not today.

Driving downtown was so nice. We have what they call a 'diamond lane' for vehicles with two or more passengers, motorcycles and buses. It is great because driving your bus in this lane you can pass most of the traffic that is creeping along on the freeway.

As I got off the freeway, and turned on to a city street, the traffic became a little congested. I let passengers off at almost every bus stop for the next three city blocks. I told everyone to enjoy their day, or have a good day, and they all responded "You to!" I was really feeling good that day. It reminded me of my driving days in sunny California where I started my bus driving career. Now I'm finishing up my career in the great Northwest.

As I was driving through the college campus, the Japanese cherry blossom trees were in full bloom. The color of the leaves was a bright pink. Just imagine that scene for a moment. Add to that the singing of birds, and the laughter and smiles of people as they went from class to class through the beautiful landscape of the college campus.

In my early years as a child there was a movie titled "Song of the South". And this movie there was a black man named Uncle Remus, and he sang a song that went like this,

"Zippadee Do Da, Zippadee A;
My Oh My, what a wonderful day;
Plenty of sunshine heading my way;

Zippadee Do Da, Zippadee A."

There is more to the song, but you get the idea.

After I deboarded all my passengers, I had a break at the end of the line. When I arrived there were already about six buses parked there. I pulled in, parked my bus, got out my seat with my wheel block in my hand and went out the door. I put my wheel block under the back tire of the bus and started walking to the coffee shop to get a snack. The walk was so refreshing and many students busy talking about all kinds of subjects. I was feeling good, married to a wonderful woman, who was the fulfillment of my dream, eight healthy children and a job that I really didn't seem like it was a job, because I liked it so much. It was just fun to me. I enjoy driving and I like people. I had no idea what was about to happen on my route.

As I left the coffee shop with a cinnamon roll, I said, "Hi." to some bus drivers as I walked by. I picked up my wheel block and boarded my bus. I started my route through the campus picking up people along the way who were finished for the day and going home. In about ten minutes my bus was half full. After I got through the campus I turned right on a city street to pick up more passengers. As I picked up passengers at one stop, I automatically looked ahead at the next bus stop to see who was there to be picked up. Sometimes there may be a passenger in a wheelchair waiting to be picked up. If there happened to be someone sitting in the seats of the bus where I have to tie the wheelchair down, I would ask them politely to move.

At the next bus stop, suddenly a young man, who was standing up, fell down and began to shake violently on the ground. Just before I stopped the bus next to him, he got up off the ground, dusted himself off, and got on the bus. To my amazement and to everybody who heard him, he said, "I'm sorry."

I answered, "For what?"

He said, "My medication for my epileptic condition has run out and I'm on my way to get it refilled at the doctor."

I told him to sit down in the front seat near me. He agreed and sat down. Showing my concern for him, I asked him how long he had this condition. He told me he had been this way since he was seven years old and he was now 31 years old.

He also told me that he was helping his mother was take care of three little babies that were addicted to drugs because their mothers were taking drugs while they were carrying them. I shook my head in disbelief.

Because I have a tender heart for children, I can't see how anyone can put a child at risk because of their irresponsible behavior. I don't want to be judgmental but children and babies need someone to take care of them and not have their lives put in danger. If one can't take care of them, give them to someone who can love them and take care of them. Excuse me for getting emotional. We all came into this world as a baby and we have a right to live and not be destroyed because of someone's selfishness or because the baby is inconvenient.

Getting back to the young man, can you guess what happened next? You are right. The Holy Spirit spoke to my heart telling me to ask the young man if he wanted to be healed of this condition. So I asked him. The young man said he did, with a surprised look on his face.

Then the Holy Spirit told me to ask him if people had made fun of him because of this epileptic condition? After I asked him this, he again said, "Yes."

The Holy Spirit said in my spirit to tell him that God would heal him but first he would have to *forgive* all of those people who have made fun of him. He would have to be sincere for God to heal him. Again I explained what he must do and he looked at me with tears in his eyes. I told him to pray quietly asking God to help him forgive those people and He would help him to forgive them. The young man quietly prayed as we continued on the route.

What I didn't expect was what the Holy Spirit told me to do next. He wanted me to lay hands on the young man and He would heal him. I was shocked and scared. I had almost a bus load of people going down the freeway.

"Surely, God, you don't want me to do this? I can't do this on the bus." I thought. What I forgot was I can't heal anybody. It's one's faith and the power of the Holy Spirit that brings healing. God uses people as instruments to perform the miracles.

As time went on we arrived at his bus stop. By then I had seven people left on the bus. In obedience to the Holy Spirit, I got out of my seat and said to the people, "I have a brother sitting here who needs help. Please be patient for a few minutes."

They sat with a dazed look in their eyes. They didn't know what was going to happen. I stood over the young man with my right hand resting on top of his head and began to pray the prayer of faith to cast out the epileptic spirit in him and set him free. He agreed with me and said he accepted the healing. Within a few moments he sat upright in his seat. Then suddenly he jumped up shouting, "I'm free. I'm free." He jumped off the bus and kept shouting. He turned, thanked me for caring about him, and walked off to his destination.

When I sat down again, in my mirror I saw the other passengers on the bus sitting still like they were frozen. They didn't know what had happened. Almighty God had healed that man who was in bondage for 24 years. Now he was set free.

This can happen for you to. No matter what you need in your life, there is nothing to big for God. And there is nothing to small either. Call on Him and be helped.

LET THE HOLY SPIRIT LEAD

This story taught me a valuable lesson about the Holy Spirit. In the Bible it says that the Holy Spirit will guide you into all truth. (John 16:13) The key word in this statement is *guide.* The Holy Spirit will not push you. Satan will push you to do things you know that you should not do. But you know what people say, "If it feels good do it!" Nowhere in the Bible have I read where God says to do what He wants you to do, *if you feel like it!* Please don't get me wrong. God has created us with feelings; but God doesn't want us to let our feelings dictate our lives.

Let me ask you this, how many times in your

life have you gotten up in the morning, but you really didn't feel like getting up? You would rather stay in bed, but you made your body get up and begin your day's work. For a mother it may be to help her small children or a husband to get ready for work or a child getting ready for school. Responsibility will get you moving.

How many times have you done something wrong and you knew it was wrong while you were doing it; but you let your feelings drive you. I have learned to do what's right *first*, and let your feelings follow you. Let this story explain how this works.

When a driver arrives at a park and ride lot where passengers transfer to another bus, there is usually time for the drivers get a rest break before they begin the next route. For other drivers, their routes end there and they drive with no one on the bus in what we call a "deadhead" route to another location to start a new route.

Today I was driving one of those long extended buses. We call them "articulated" coaches. Since my next route started downtown at the university, I would drive a "deadhead" route there. It would take about twenty minutes.Well after I had let off all my passengers and was ready to take off, a young man saw me pulling away in the bus and banged on the side of the bus with his fist, wanting me to stop. I stopped the bus. He asked me if I was I going downtown and if he could get a ride?

I said, "Sure, come on."

He was dirty, skinny and looked like he had been sleeping outside somewhere. He told me he didn't have any money. The expression on his face was sad and very tired. Seeing the young man in this condition I wanted to help him. Having compassion for him, I wanted him to sit up front so I could minister to him telling him about Jesus and how He loved him, and died for him so he could be free from sadness. But when he walked on the bus he went straight to the back of the bus and sat down. He just looked out the window like he didn't know what to do or where he was going.

After looking in my rear view mirror, just when I was about to call him up to the front, the Holy Spirit spoke to me quietly and said, "No!" Immediately I began to question this in my mind. Maybe this was the devil trying to stop me. I could see that this young man needed help. So why was I told not to help him? I was about to learn a great lesson.

Driving along still a little bit confused, the Holy Spirit put in my spirit that when the young man got up to leave, I was to give him five dollars, tell him Jesus loves him and He had told me to give this money to him.

Sure enough after I turned off the freeway and entered the local street, the young man rang the bell to get off at the next stop. The bus I was driving had three exit doors, two in the back, and one in the front. While watching him and opening all three doors, I'm thinking to myself that, with him sitting in the far back of the bus, he won't walk all the way up to the front to exit because he has two doors in the back through which to exit before he gets to me. How wrong I was! He got up and walked past the two open doors right up to me. I set the brake and got up out of my seat. I pulled out a five dollar bill, put it in his hand, and started talking to him. I told him exactly what the Holy Spirit told me to tell him. He was trembling and tears began to fall down his cheeks. With his head lowered he said, "Thank you. Thank you very much." The young man left the bus and walked down the street. I knew in his heart he realized that someone cared about him.

What's the lesson here? No matter how anxious you are to minister to someone because of the way you feel or by what you see, it may be the right thing to do, but the wrong time to do it. The Holy Spirit knew that the young man didn't need any preaching to right then. He needed someone just to care about him. If I had started preaching to him, it would have turned him off to the things of God. The Holy Spirit knew the young man's heart was not receptive right then and wanted me to learn to be patient. It's not me that does the work to change lives. It's the power of the Holy Spirit that convicts the heart. Then the new birth comes through the salvation of Jesus Christ.

Remember the Holy Spirit is here to *guide* us. Don't jump ahead of Him. The Bible says He is here to guide us, teach us, to tell of things to come, and to keep us in the remembrance of our Lord Jesus Christ. The Holy Spirit is a gentle person. Get to know Him. (John 16:7:16)

"SATAN, BE QUIET."

This story will show the reader the powerful word of God. I had a chance to do this with a threat on my life. Let me tell you that the night before this particular day, my wife and I were watching Christian television. On this program the preacher was explaining the power that the Christian believer has. He was saying that the believer can speak in other tongues, lay hands on the sick and they shall recover, eat or drink anything deadly, and by no means shall anything harm us. (Mark 16:15-18) Plus we can even cast out demons because, being born again, we have the Holy Spirit in us to lead us. He went on to say that we are children of the King, who is God. The preacher said that when anyone asked us who we were, we should answer, "I am a child of the King."

As I was watching and listening, I said to myself, "Wow!" I already spoke in tongues and know the Bible teaches that speaking in tongues will build you up. (I Corinthians 14:4) I said aloud to my wife," Next time someone asks me who I am, I am going to say, "I'm a child of the King." I had no idea that the next day I would be tested. Let me show you what happened to me.

Around noon the next day, it was bright and sunny. I was coming into town with a load of passengers. The bus was full because it was the time of the month when there were reduced sales at the department stores downtown. My passengers were mostly women with babies, desiring to pickup some good deals. I was feeling good, especially since at the end of this route I would get about a 15 minute break.

After all my passengers left the bus, I turned off the engine, picked up my wheel block, and got out of the bus. The bus was parked on a hill so I blocked the wheel for safety reasons. The sidewalk was clear of people and I saw no one. I had a nice big peach that I was going to eat on my break. I was getting ready to bite into it when I heard a loud voice behind me say, "Who do you think you are? I'm going to kill you, you blank, blank, son of a blank." He just starred at me with a mean expression on his face.

As I turned around cold chills went up my back. There stood a man that looked to be about seven feet tall and at least 280 hundred pounds. (I am 6' 1" tall.) My first thought was that I would have to fight this guy physically or he would attack me and kill me. There was nobody around to call for help. Then I was reminded if I get into a fight on the job, I could be fired. I had a wife and children to help support so I couldn't fight this guy. As my mind raced to find an answer for him, I remembered the preacher's message last night, and I answered him, "I am a child of the King."

Then suddenly the voice of the Holy Spirit told me to cast out the demon in this man. I knew I had the power to do it. What a challenge I faced at that moment. Knowing that the Holy Spirit knew all truth, I also knew that He would not ask me to do anything that I could not do. So, in obedience to the Holy Spirit, I boldly walked straight up to this huge man and said to him in a loud voice, with the authority Jesus said in Mark 16:17 that all believers have, "In the name of Jesus Christ , Satan come out of him."

Immediately, the mean and angry expression on his face was replaced with a calm expression.

I got really close to him, put my left hand on his right shoulder, and asked him, "What's wrong?"

Tears began to run down his face as he said, "I have been in a hospital and they were using me for a guinea pig." He told me his name and explained that a nearby hospital was experimenting on him with drugs and needles and he was in great pain. Feeling compassion for him, I prayed with him right there on the street to break the power of Satan over him and for him to be set free. Continuing on, I asked God to heal his pains and help him to find new life in Jesus Christ.

"Thank you," he said peacefully and turned and walked away before I could say any more. It was like he felt peaceful that someone cared about him to take the time listen to him and to pray with him. This was a real test for me to see what I would do when confronted with danger.

Let me say this to you who are reading this,

there is no victory without a battle;
there is no testimony without a test!

When you are faced with danger, speak the Word of God and you will overcome the danger. God has said in his Word, "For God has not given us a spirit of fear, but of power, and of love, and of a sound mind. Therefore do not be ashamed of the testimony of our Lord..." I Timothy 1:7-8

DESPAIR REVERSED

In this story you will see that the feeling of being defeated is only in one's assumption. This proves that if you know better, you can do better. The Bible states it this way in Hosea 4:6. God says, "My people are destroyed for lack of knowledge." On the other hand, "Happy is the man (or woman) who finds wisdom, and gains understanding." (Proverbs 3:13) God teaches you this principle in many more scriptures in the Bible. Now let's get on with this story to see how this works.

As I previously stated, a bus driver has a chance to change routes from time to time. On my new route I took many students to a community college. My bus was so full that many had to stand up on the way to school. Over time, I struck up conversations with some of them. Many of them seem happy and excited during the first days and weeks of school. But near graduation, something happened. I began to see fear and sadness on the faces of some of those who used to have big smiles and sunny disposition. What happened? Despair had set in their hearts because they were not doing well enough to pass their classes to earn the degree that they studied for. Some were financially supported by their families, some got into college by grants, and some had to pay out of their own pockets, which can be quite a sum.

As a driver and Christian I have compassion for those who are depressed and living in fear of defeat. Because I know that there is nothing, *nothing,* impossible with God, there is hope for anyone who feels defeated. Call on God and pray for help. He will hear you and answer you, if you believe. He doesn't care if you are old or young, black or white, rich or poor. When you call on Him sincerely in faith, He promises you shall be saved. One particular thing I like about God; when you call on him, He doesn't put you on hold and play music to you while you wait like some businesses do. You know what I'm talking about. Are you ready to see the Holy

Spirit work again? I thought you were.

The young lady in this story, who by the way, is an American Indian is a small framed young lady with dark red hair. She was quiet and reserved, but she did feel at ease talking to me because I was willing to listen. She explained the subjects that she was taking and how she would use them to further her knowledge. She told me she was trying to succeed in educating herself for a better life.

One day, when she got on the bus at the college to go home, she was crying. I asked her what was wrong. She explained she was failing one of her classes. Her grades were to low, and if she didn't raise her grades up, her teacher told her he couldn't pass her. She was so disappointed because she was trying so hard to learn. I told her that we were going to pray to God that He would help her get her diploma. At her bus stop there was only one person on the bus beside her. I set the brake and prayed with her that she would pass her classes. At the same time, I quietly asked the Holy Spirit to help me to tell her what to do.

Then I told her that she was going about it the wrong way. Let's see what God tells us to do in the Bible. In Mark 11:24, Jesus is speaking and says, "Therefore I say to you, whatever things you ask when you pray, believe that you receive them, and you will have them." I explained to her that this was the answer to her problem.

She asked how this verse worked. Explaining to her, I told her that she had worked hard thinking that she had to pass this course to get that diploma. But Jesus said," to believe that you receive (already have it now) them." I asked her how she would feel with the diploma in her hand being congratulated by the dean. Her face lit up with a big smile, and she said, "Why, I would feel great!"

I told her to see herself receiving her diploma from your teacher *now* before she actually got it! Jesus calls this Faith. Continuing on, I told her just before she went to bed at night, pray and thank God for the diploma she had received. I told her that if she believed in her heart without doubt, she would have what she has asked for. Then getting the good grades would come along to make the diploma happen. I believe at that moment the Holy Spirit touched her and she really believed. Her attitude had changed. She began to look at the classes as stepping stones toward that diploma.

In the following weeks it proved to be true. She passed all of her classes and received her diploma. She was so excited and thanked me.

She also asked me for my address so she could write me and tell me how she and her husband were doing. She told me her husband, who also was an American Indian, was struggling trying to get a job at a near-by factory. She told him about God, and how she had prayed and received help in getting her diploma, but he did not want to hear it. He didn't trust Christians and their God. I told her to just pray for him and believe that he would eventually trust God.

One Christmas we got a letter from her telling us that she and her husband were moving to a new apartment and were doing well. Several more years passed before I heard from her again. This time she and her husband had a baby and asked if I would pray for her and her family. I said I would be glad to. What I didn't know was that the Holy Spirit was working in their marriage.

Then last year, a letter came from her with a picture of her, her husband, and a little boy. She and her husband wanted to know if they could come to our church, and have our pastor dedicate their baby. My wife and I both read this letter together and almost began to shout!! One thing I have learned, if I plant the seed, God will do the changing.

The lady, her husband, and precious baby

came to our church where their baby, among others was dedicated. After talking to both of them we found out that they both had given their lives to Christ, and had joined a good Christian church, the same church the lady in the "Eight Years of Pain" story attended. The pastor and people of their church were so friendly to them and were helping them with their marriage. Praise the Lord!

Oh I almost forgot; my wife and I were invited to come to their church for their baby's second dedication. Maybe this is what the Bible calls this a double portion! There is nothing, *no-thing*, impossible WITH GOD.

LISTEN FOR GOD'S VOICE

This next story is a revelation to many Christians who always desire to give to the poor. It shows how important it is to listen to God's voice, and be prepared for His guidance. Jesus said himself in John 5:30, "...I do not seek My own will but the will of the Father who sent Me." The Bible clearly states that the Holy Spirit is given to us, to ..."guide us into all truth." (John 16:13) We are not to go ahead of Him but to let Him lead us. How does this work? Well let's find out.

Some people are poor and need help. Others are poor and just want to stay that way and beg.

Some want to do better in life and some don't. I have worked since I was seven years old and I respect all who work. The Bible even says, "If anyone will not work, neither shall he eat." (II Thessalonians 3:10)

Quite tough, you may think.

When I was a little boy walking down the street in town with my Mother and Dad, we saw a blind man on the street with a cup asking for money. My Mother and Dad felt sorry for him and gave him some money. We were shopping that evening and continued walking along looking at all the nice things in the stores.

We went down a few blocks and came back the same way about an hour later. As we walked by this bar where people were drinking beer, the door of the place was wide open because it was very hot that evening. Guess what we saw? The man we thought was blind was sitting on a bar stool drinking. I saw him first and grabbed my Mother's coat and told her to look because there was the blind man to whom we gave the money. She looked into the bar at the same time Dad did and they saw him. A funny thing happened; the so-called blind man turned and looked out the door at us, as if he could feel someone was looking at him. Mother, Dad and I just shook our heads in disbelief. He looked so ashamed when he saw us. I have never forgotten that event.

After my experience as a child, I was always very skeptical of people on the streets who asked for money. Although I have given money to people on the street many times, a few years ago when a man on the street asked me for some money I told him I knew where he could find a job. He shook his head "No." and walked away. He didn't want a job to earn the money.

When I grew as a Christian I found out that God, through the Holy Spirit, wants to lead us to give to the poor. We should not give out of our guilt. Sometimes we feel that we need to give to others because we think we need to do something to please God. This amounts to 'works'; in other words, working for our salvation.

I was listening to a preacher talk on television one day, and he said he had been giving to the poor on the street for years, but one day just after he had given money to a poor man on the street, a voice in his spirit asked him why he gave his money to this man? This shocked the preacher, because he thought this was what he was supposed to do. Then he got the revelation. The Holy Spirit in his heart said, "I didn't tell you to give money to him."

You may ask, "Why not?" Well I have learned

what the preacher has learned; that if we keep giving to people without teaching them about Jesus, they will stay in poverty. Jesus has come to set us free from the curse of the law which is poverty, sickness, and premature death. (Deuteronomy 28:15-67 and Galatians 3:13) If we don't teach the poor how to succeed in getting out of poverty, giving them money will only help to keep them down. They need to be taught about Jesus so they can allow Him to help them out of poverty. Can you see this clearly now?

Let me show you how this worked for me on this day. Another day out on the road driving the bus I saw many kinds of people. My route was about 45 minutes one way. I drove this route for eight hours, so I saw the same things more than once.

This day I saw a young man standing on the corner of a block with a sign saying, "I need money and will work." When I first saw him, I said to myself why doesn't he go look for a job? I drove my route back and forth many times that day and tried not to look at him as I went by him. I really didn't want to see him. I wanted him to go away, but he didn't. You can imagine what happened next?

The Holy Spirit began to speak to my heart. This is what He said. Listen carefully!! He told me to give the young man some money and tell him that I would pray for him to get a job that he wanted and that would pay him the hourly wage he wanted. But he must believe that Jesus is the one that will make it happen.

After my heart received the word from the Holy Spirit, I made the round trip again, but this time as I was turning the corner I looked straight at him and blew the horn. Stopping the bus, I motioned for him to come into the bus. He saw me and came over to the bus. As I opened the door and let him in, I told him to stand right there by me and listen. I got some money out of my pocket and gave it to him and said, "The Lord told me to give you this money."

He took it and thanked me. Then I asked him what kind of job he wanted and how much money he wanted to make per hour? He told me the kind of job he wanted and added that he wanted to make at least seven dollars an hour so he could take care of his family. I told him that I would pray for him to get the job he wanted and would ask God to give him seven dollars an hour. When I said that, a great big smile came on his face. As he stepped off the bus, the last thing I said to him was, "Go find that job. It's waiting for you." He waved good bye to me and left.

It's amazing how a person can change if they

can see a way out of their condition. The words that I spoke to him were not from me. It was the Holy Spirit speaking to him through me. When I got to the end of my route I prayed for him just as the Holy Spirit told me to. Do you think my prayer was answered? Jesus often said to believe and fear not. I believed, and if the man believed, it would happen.

A few weeks later, I was driving my bus on the same route one day and pulled up to a bus stop, and guess who was standing there? That same young man was there and he jumped on the bus as I opened the door and said,

"I have been riding around on all the routes today looking for you. Another driver told me to wait right here and you would be driving the next bus to come by. I got the job I have always wanted, and I'm making seven dollars an hour!" He kept on talking about how he had been trying to catch up with me to tell me the good news and to pay me back the money I gave him. I told him to keep the money and use it for his family. He was so excited and kept thanking me for my prayers. I reminded him that it was God who had answered his prayer.

What can I say except I know and now he knows that with God <u>ALL</u>, let me say it again; "<u>FOR WITH GOD ALL THINGS ARE POSSI-</u>

BLE!!" (Mark 10:27) If you don't know Jesus you are missing out.

EPILOGUE

This is the last story in this book, but there are many more that I could tell. For all these lives to be changed, it was the love of God who sent His Son, Jesus Christ, into the World to destroy the works of the devil. The devil is the one that comes to steal, kill, and destroy our lives with ungodly behavior. I hope these true stories will help someone who doesn't really like the way their life is going and those who know that they are not living the way God created them to live.

Jesus said what no other man could say to mankind, which is to turn away from your sinful life, come unto Him and be born again. (John 3:16) It's your choice!! If you decide that you want a better life than you have now, if you are tired of being unfulfilled, angry, bitter, prejudiced, jealous, living a lifestyle of sexual immorality and you want something better, say this prayer sincerely,

"Jesus, you said if I call upon you, and ask you to forgive me of my sin, and make you my Lord and Savior, I will be saved. I want to be born again. Jesus, I believe you are the Son of the living God. I turn away and repent of my sinful ways. Cleanse me, wash me, and take away my desire to live in an ungodly way. Jesus, I thank you, and believe that I now have Salvation through Jesus Christ."

If you prayed this prayer, give Almighty God thanksgiving and praise. YOU NOW BELONG TO GOD, and the devil has no claim on your life any longer. Pray for the Holy Spirit to lead you to a good anointed church that teaches and operates in all the gifts of the Holy Spirit taught in the Bible. These gifts, when applied in your life, with faith and patience, will make you the VICTOR instead of the victim.

May God greatly bless you.

Printed in the United States
16078LVS00001B/118-177